RICHARD STEINPACH

HIDDEN CONNECTIONS DETERMINE OUR EARTH-LIFE

HIDDEN CONNECTIONS DETERMINE OUR EARTH-LIFE

THE COMING-INTO-BEING OF MAN IN THE LAW OF REBIRTH

Manuscript of a
Lecture by
Richard Steinpach
Vienna

STIFTUNG GRALSBOTSCHAFT PUBLISHING CO.
STUTTGART

ISBN 3-87860-168-9

What more is there still to be said about the coming-into-being of man? After all, we have known for a long time how man comes into being. We are enlightened, and have everything "in hand"! We can prevent the coming-into-being of man where it is not desired; on the other hand we can bring it about even where it would not normally be possible.

But it is just with regard to this latter undertaking, to test-tube fertilisation, which has been carried to the point of surrogate and rent mothers, that we find ourselves all at once confronted with a host of genetic, legal and ethical problems from which we can find no way out. We do not really feel easy about this progress. And on the other hand the warning voices against abortion will not be silenced. Very many conflicting things have been said and written about it in recent years, much that should be able to shake our arrogance.

But first let me assure you that none of the arguments from either side, which have been discussed ad nauseam, will be either repeated or added to here. Rather the fact that even today we can still hold different views about a process which has always taken place in the same way since the earliest beginning of mankind is indeed only frightening evidence of how little we really know about the whole matter. We experiment with the existence of this creature "man", without being absolutely clear about what man actually is, and what purpose this earth-life really serves.

Therefore I ask you: In the course of the numerous dissertations and discussions, have you ever received an answer to these questions? Or is it perhaps so obvious that there is no more to be said on the subject?

In 1970 the renowned biologist Ludwig von Bertalanffy gave one of his books the title: "... but of man we know nothing"; and as recently as 1984 the Salzburg Colloquium on Humanism considered the question: "What does medical science know of man?"

Our picture of man is still controversial. For – and that is ever again the salient point: Is man this physical body? But is it not striking that everyone, in speaking of this body, will say that he has a body. How naturally we separate this body from our ego, making it a possession, which is not identical with the ego. Therefore – as distinguished from the body – we speak also of a "soul". But what is this soul? What do we picture to ourselves by this catchword?

This missing dimension is now to be discussed here. Only this enables us to recognise those hidden connections that lie behind the façade of outward appearances; a façade along which we – let us be honest – proceed rather unsuspectingly and helplessly. For – unfortunately – a mystery still surrounds the coming-into-being of man. Of course it hardly concerns the physical side of our existence, but rather all that actually determines our being man. And therefore it is necessary to consider this "being man" from the *spiritual* point of view.

Of course I may be using a concept which for some of you is too vague, too meaningless and expressionless. For if you ask someone: "What exactly is spirit?" the person asked will probably be surprised at first, and then perhaps reply: "The intellect ...., reason ..." Hardly anyone will say: "It is I myself!" And so you see that our whole human tragedy lies in this non-recognition of our own species. The creature man has lived on this planet for thousands of years – and still largely belies himself, because the intellectual play, the fostering of doubt, is more important to him than the call from his inner being. Yet so long as man does not have clarity about himself he lacks the starting-point of all his deliberations. For he is not then in a position to judge what is really of benefit to him, that is in accordance with the purpose of his existence.

Therefore let it be made absolutely clear at once that our innermost core, our actual ego, is *spirit*. But please do not confuse this concept with worldly cleverness, with the intellect. The intellect, which so often we take to be the spirit – as for example we describe purely intellectual activity as "spiritual work" – this intellect is but a data bank for information, a calculating machine which can be imitated by the computer for purely earthly purposes. In sober, matter-of-fact thought-processes, as in technology, it is capable of notable achievements. But just as a computer is tied to the substance of the machine, the so-called hardware, so the intellect requires the material instrument of the brain. The spirit, however, is of a totally different, non-material species.

You may perhaps wish to say: "Well, that is just an assertion. But where is the proof?" May I say something fundamental to you about this: Only earthly things can be proved by material means; Truth, which transcends the boundaries of matter, never! I also want to tell you why this is so and can never be otherwise. By "proving" we surely mean making it possible for our senses to investigate something. But these senses are sight, hearing, smell, taste and touch. They are all bound to our physical body. Yet it is just the extra-sensory that cannot be grasped in this way, any more than water can be drawn with a net. At best a few drops will be caught in it. In relation to our subject, these are then perhaps the results of parapsychology. In this way there can never be any true drawing, any gaining of recognition.

Only in spirit can you experience proof of the spirit. And there you will actually find it; for you bear it within you. In science there is the so-called "information theory". This is a rather high-sounding term for what is basically a very simple fact, such as that two litres cannot be poured into a one-litre container. Or expressed in different, more general terms, that nothing can reach beyond itself, beyond the boundaries set by its species. But then you are actually able to grasp, to perceive intuitively, and to experience love and hate, joy and sorrow, beauty, gratitude, in short extra-material values. And in this, in the sense of scientific information theory, lies the proof that you bear within you what is extra-material, for otherwise you would lack the ability to comprehend it.

Even distinguished scientists are today no longer afraid of calling this spirit by name. Thus for example the brain scientist, Nobel Prize-winner Sir John Eccles writes in his book "The Self and Its Brain":

*"As a neuronal machine the brain in principle cannot perform the necessary integration (this refers to the grasping of all those things that constitute our being man). An active and independent spirit, which makes use of the brain as an instrument, is needed for this."**

This insight by a scientist precisely confirms that demand which has all along been made in the Book *"In the Light of Truth"*, The Grail Message by Abd-ru-shin. There it says:

"We must at last learn to distinguish between the spirit and the intellect, the vital core of man and his tool!"

This extra-material core, the spirit, is enveloped by several increasingly denser coverings. For we know that material substance, which appears so solid to our sen-

* co-authored with Karl Popper

ses, has issued from radiation, which becoming ever denser suddenly enters our material world. Yet what is it other than the envelopment with coverings, through that wonderful attraction-power called energy, which constitutes the innermost of every elementary particle? This, in basic principle, is a very similar process.

And in this earthly world do we not also wear coverings of varying density, depending on the conditions in which we find ourselves at the time? A shirt or a blouse, a suit or a dress, and finally an overcoat? And the less light and heat there is, the denser and heavier these coverings become. Therefore the human spirit here, far away from the radiant starting-point of Creation, also wears the densest covering, the physical body.

And this already brings us to one of the most portentous causes of our lack of understanding. For medical science is still primarily occupied with this "winter coat" of the spirit. Although it is conversant with the psychosomatic concept, that is to say the interdependence between soul (psyche) and body (soma), it only senses that there is something which goes beyond the material. To science this is – as Arthur Koestler once mockingly put it – the "ghost in the machine", which because it cannot be grasped is uncanny, and which is behind the mechanical and chemical processes.

And it is precisely this "ghost in the machine", that cannot be grasped with material means, which is the *spirit.*

When it bears a covering of fine material substance, this form of appearance can be called "soul", as distinct from the spirit itself. Hence soul – and here I am following the explanation that is given to us in the Book "In the Light of Truth" – is by no means something vague and indeterminate. It is the spirit in a covering of fine material substance. But since Nature makes no leaps, and always only one step follows the other, this "soul" just mentioned is connected with the physical body through a covering of already denser material substance, the astral body. At the same time this astral body acts as a bridge. Like a mould, it is so to speak the model for the physical body.

And now, please imagine these cloaks pushed into one another, rather like a telescope, and connected with each other through radiation.

Science has long since verified this. The elementary particles of which our material substance is composed are not perhaps mechanically connected, locked in position, or screwed together. Between them lie vast distances, which are bridged solely by radiation. Radiation holds the Universe together. Each object radiates in its own characteristic way. We can determine its condition from the nature of this radiation. What we regard as colour is the reflected radiation of light. Invisible heat-radiation can be captured through infra-red photography. We make the radiation of our vital processes visible in the form of the brain-current. During sleep this radiation, the brain-current, is decisively reduced – and at death it ceases altogether. And that proves that the holding fast of the soul, its connection with the physical body, has to do with this radiation, is dependent upon it.

I do not wish to enlarge on that for the purpose of this lecture. I have gone into the subject at great length in another lecture, entitled "How is it that we Live after Death…".*

So I would like to conclude this chapter with a sentence which comes from no less a person than the famous physicist Max Planck, who openly acknowledged his realisation:

"The actual, the real, the true, is not visible and transient material substance, but the invisible, immortal spirit."

Finally, I would ask all those who are not yet satisfied with these inevitably brief references to admit the existence of the spirit as a working-hypothesis – at least for the time being – in order to understand what follows. –

Now you will probably want to ask: If then our innermost core is spirit, and spirit is something extra-material, for what purpose are we actually here on earth in material substance? To this also we need to know the answer, where the coming-into-being of man is concerned. For does not this coming-into-being of man become meaningless if we cannot say what purpose is really served by being man? And therefore in the course of our consideration we must actually deal with that first.

For instance, what will you tell your child if – and this is by no means so unusual – one day he asks reproachfully: "Why did you bring me into this world? I certainly did not ask you to!"

Yet the answer is very simple. It is: development. And every earth-life is nothing

* If you are interested, you may obtain a free copy of the booklet containing the text of this lecture from The Grail Foundation of Great Britain, 23 Hamilton Road, Sidcup, Kent, Great Britain, DA15 7HB.

but an opportunity for this, an opportunity for the further development of each individual human spirit.

Just let us look at the history of this planet: It took millions of years for it to condense out of cosmic nebulae, to allow those compounds to arise from the primeval element hydrogen which initially became the foundation of plant life. And the latter gradually evolved from the simplest, least demanding forms, from lichens, mosses and algae, to the point where it could offer the basis of existence to animal life. This animal life too, starting with the simplest organisms from out of the primeval water of the sea, over long periods of time, through the evolutionary stages of fish and amphibian, finally conquered the land. All this lay in readiness in the radiation of the Creator-Power, the Primordial Energy, but – and this is a very important aspect – it could always only be "recalled" from there little by little when in each case, through similarity, the precondition was created for the connection with the next higher.

The human form is characteristic of the human spirit, that is to say, the spirit moulds its coverings – whether ethereal or astral in nature – always in the fashion known to us here as the physical body. Therefore to enable the human spirit to gain a foothold here on this earth, that body-form which came closest to this human body had to be brought to the highest possible degree of perfection. This was the body of the anthropoid ape. Only then could the inert, still unawakened *human spirit*, awaiting its development, appear as something *completely new* here, in order to effect the further development of this animal form into the human being wherever it had been sunk into such an animal body. From then on the ways parted. This is where man's own path of development begins, for this was – of course not just in one single creature – the first coming-into-being of man on earth.

But note the crucial precondition for the incarnation of the spirit: The vessel to receive it, the material form, had to mature towards the spirit, so to speak, in order to bring about its entry. I specially emphasise this, because we shall encounter this requirement again later on. This joining of what is relatively similar – on the one hand the most highly developed animal form nearest to man, on the other the still undeveloped human spirit – is what obscures the boundary, because the new does not yet stand out enough. And that is why science too is hardly in a position to classify the various discoveries of bones, and state categorically which was still animal and which was already man.

Hence the Darwinian theory of the origin of the species is both right and wrong.

It is true with regard to the body-covering, but it overlooks the fact that through the spirit a completely *new motivating impetus to further development* was added. The assertion that man is descended from the ape is just like trying to say that the motor car is descended from the horse-drawn vehicle because like the latter it has wheels and is a means of transport. We would smile at such an assertion, for we know that the engine makes all the difference, and that this completely dissimilar kind of motive-power facilitates performance that no horse-drawn vehicle would be able to achieve. And just as the motor car has developed from the first vehicles that chugged slowly along, right up to the modern fast racing cars, so the human spirit also has continued to develop away from its early forms to that being who has brought forth all the achievements which are summed up in the concept "culture", and which are yet true accomplishments of the spirit.

And with each birth this evolutionary history of the species is repeated in quick tempo, as it were: To begin with the embryo develops hints of gills, then an amphibious tail, and finally a fur covering. Hence each one undergoes once more in a condensed form the material-animal sequence of evolution; and mankind's early stages of consciousness which once embraced hundreds of thousands of years, the slow process of orientation in this earthly world, are today compressed into childhood. And even this childhood is becoming shorter and shorter, the young are maturing ever earlier. You see, although we build up on the preceding development, the freedom at our disposal to continue this development is growing steadily, so that we can add new aspects to it. There is an acceleration, a certain urgency in this happening. And after all, this is significant!

But in what does this development consist? We are in the habit of saying apologetically "No one is perfect," and with that we hit exactly upon the right thing. For man from his earliest beginnings is and remains a learner. He is by no means conscious yet of his abilities, his possibilities and requirements, for the human spirit is only a *spirit-germ*. Like the shoot of a plant, it needs external influences to develop the talents resting within it. With the plant it is the soil, sun, wind and weather which further its growth; with man it is joy and sorrow, in short it is experience that helps him to mature. For just as physically we could not place one foot in front of the other if there were no friction, so too does the spirit need "friction" with the environment, that is, contact and coming-to-terms with it, in order to advance; for

"Life learns from itself – through continuous feedback",

that is how the biologist Professor Rupert Riedl outlines the essence of evolution. And this process is certainly not over yet. Each man continues it for himself, for his spirit. The ongoing development of spiritual talents is indeed nothing but the continuation of what we have recognised in material substance as "evolution", namely the bringing forth of increasingly mature manifestations. And that very process of learning which lay at the root of this development, namely the ever-improving adaptation – enforced by the reciprocal action – to the realities of the environment, as determined by the Laws of Nature, is also the means to spiritual progress. Experiencing is to man that "feedback", which brings him the answer to his volition and deed, and thereby helps him to maturing realisation. The ancient folk-wisdom "practice is better than theory" says exactly the right thing. The accumulation of knowledge acquired by study, hence which is lifeless, is of no benefit to the spirit. Only experience which has been assimilated, and through the reciprocal action is filled with life, is of benefit.

And now please consider: What happens for example when an apprentice joins a firm? How does his training proceed? He will first come to know his more immediate sphere of activity; he will have to begin by training his abilities, developing them further, to enable him to use them effectively. Gradually he will learn also to understand the interaction among the departments, and discover the significance of his activity within the framework of the whole.

And if he then wishes to grow into ever higher tasks, he will have to pay attention to the economic rules and regulations, and appreciate that only those products which are of use to the buyer will find a market. The understanding that arises from this is simply that his own profit is dependent on the benefit he provides for others through his activity.

All this really seems rather obvious to us. But note here how much we follow, indeed must follow, the rules that govern our own course of development. For the Laws of Creation remain ever the same – in great things as well as in small. They merely manifest in the various spheres of activity in a way that is characteristic of these spheres.

Just like an apprentice, the human spirit too once began his development. He has just reached the stage at which he knows how to make use of some of his abilities – not always very skilfully either. He still lacks understanding of the connections, of how to fit his activities into the great, complete whole. This applies not only with regard to the earthly, where even today the ecological problems demonstrate quite clearly to us this lack of understanding, but to a far greater extent with regard to our place and task in Creation.

Man the apprentice often acts like an immature youth, who – instead of concerning himself with the far away goal of his ascent – leads a carefree existence with only his comfort, his well-being and his pleasures in mind. For that is precisely what we do when we put our extremely short-term imaginary advantages in first place, and do not ask what will benefit our spiritual development.

For we should long since have become conscious of the essence of our apprenticeship. The main point is to recognise the Laws of this Creation, into which we are placed as a co-operating part because of the influence exerted by this part. The religions are no longer needed today to remind us of this responsibility; the natural sciences already see to that. So for example the famous science journalist Hoimar von Ditfurth writes:

> *"One of the most exciting results of modern science is the fact that from the vast number of individual results produced by it there begins to emerge ever more clearly, as though fitted together from countless mosaic pieces, the picture of a world in which everything is interconnected, the greatest with the smallest, the nearest with the furthest...... A united, integrated world." ("Wir sind nicht nur von dieser Welt" – "We are not only of this World", Hoffman und Campe/Hamburg)*

and the well-known biochemist and environmentalist Frederic Vester actually completes this with the words:

> *"When all at once it was established that every system projects into another, that not a single one exhausts itself in its own sphere of life, it became clear that here too there could be no separate rules." ("Neuland des Denkens". DVA "Breaking New Ground for Thought").*

And now I ask you to consider the full significance of this statement! There can be no separate rules! Everything is subject to the same Laws! We are no exception either!

Within their limitations, the latest scientific findings here confirm the Grail Message, in which it had long ago been stated:

"There always rests in everything only the same simple Law! In the finest spiritual as in the coarsest earthly. Without change and without deviation. It takes effect and must be observed."

We have to fit in with these rules. For they form the framework of our existence. And since we as spiritual creatures are capable of and destined for conscious activity, this fitting in must also be done consciously, that is *knowingly.* With the plant and the animal, evolution, as we have had to discover, has always ensured that whatever was not adapted to its living conditions died out, was eliminated, became extinct. How can we assume that it would be any different with us? This is slowly beginning to dawn on us in connection with the manifold environmental problems.

In our small daily affairs we have long since been practising these realisations. What would you tell your little son if he failed to solve his mathematics exercise correctly, if for example he calculated 3 x 3 = 8? However much he pleads and begs: "Dad, I really tried to do everything correctly; please let 3 x 3 be 8!", you will nevertheless have to say to him: "My dear child, I am sorry, but there is no haggling or quibbling. The laws of mathematics are simply immovable. You will just have to do the exercise again, for exercises have to be practised until they are mastered!"

If you, as a responsible parent with his child's progress at heart, were to speak thus in such a case, you would, strictly speaking, have thereby acknowledged and put into practice two recognitions which are of vast importance for your whole existence. Firstly: You have found out that there are rules which are immovable, before which there can be only "right" or "wrong". And exactly that applies to the Laws of Creation, for which mathematics is simply a means of making them comprehensible.

And secondly: in demanding that the wrongly-solved problem be repeated you have recognised the purpose of rebirth, of reincarnation, which is still a mystery to many people; and moreover you have realised the need for it! For rebirth is indeed the grace that allows us to atone for mistakes made and to go on learning, since the subject matter which we are permitted to acquire can as little be grasped in one life as your son would have exhausted the whole subject of mathematics even if he had rightly calculated 3 x 3 = 9. So you see, it is for this reason that so many people cling to life on earth, thinking that there is still so much to be made use of and experienced. They quite rightly perceive intuitively the magnitude of the not yet mastered task.

Reincarnation certainly makes it possible for us to continue this learning process. But just as in the end a pupil must be rejected if, despite all the re-examinations offered to him, he fails to reach the required standard, so too is the possibility for our spiritual development, which must first take place here in the dense World of Matter, limited by the state of ripeness of this planet. Astrophysics recognised only a few decades ago what we have long since been told in the Work "In the Light of Truth", namely that each heavenly body passes through a cycle of development and dissolution.

Nevertheless we should not imagine that this end lies in the unforeseeable future. Consider: Millions of years passed before man could establish himself on this earth. Going by the assertions of science that even our central star, the sun, will one day blow up into a red giant and finally cave in on itself in a gravitational collapse, it does not take much imagination to assume that already long before that human life, bound as it is to very definite and critical conditions, will no longer be possible on this planet. Moreover, through his behaviour man is zealously attempting to render the earth uninhabitable long before that. From this you can realise the clearly discernible limitation that is set to our spirit's possibility of maturing even in the course of rebirths. For by then the spirit must already have had all those experiences which it can only have in material substance, and which it absolutely needs for its maturing. Through these it must in good time have so grown in strength – that is, become conscious of its possibilities and tasks within the framework of Creation – that it can exist as spirit in the extra-material worlds without still needing the support of material substance. This is the same Law, but obviously in much greater dimension, that we can also observe here in the earthly world: for the child too, on attaining adulthood, must be able to do without parental care if it does not wish to become unfit for life; the fruit also must detach itself from the tree after the period allotted for its ripening, otherwise it would decay.

But perhaps you may still think: "Reincarnation – again, that is only conjecture! Would I not already know something about it, if I am supposed to have lived a number of times before?" Well, this allegedly most weighty argument, which has ever and again been put forward to refute reincarnation, has after all long ago been invalidated by science. For we know today that everything we retain in our memory for longer than about twenty minutes – the so-called "long-term memory" – comes into being through the forming and storing of protein compounds in the brain. But this brain – like the whole body – decays after earthly death. With rebirth we receive a new body and with it also a new brain, in whose day-conscious memory there cannot logically be contained those protein compounds which were once formed in another brain. For this new brain is like an unrecorded magnetic tape. If you buy such a new, unrecorded cassette, you do not expect to rediscover on it a recording you made previously on another. Therefore the experiences, the lessons of former existences cannot be found in our day-conscious memory. But they have entered into our spirit, into our personality. They determine the character, the abilities and the talents which we bring with us even at birth, as the formative result of our previous existences and journeyings. And at times some faint memory of past lives flashes in the spirit as the impression of "déja vu", something seen before, which we cannot associate with the present earthly life.

And consider: The very fact that this review is generally hidden from us is indeed a grace, which enables us to confront unburdened by the past those situations and persons with whom we may be linked by certain ill-fated entanglements from previous lives. Redemption is thereby made easier for us.

In this connection let me immediately deal with a second argument which is always cited against reincarnation: How is it that formerly so few and now so many people live on earth? Where then have all these human spirits come from, if they are supposed to have lived several times before? Well, to this also the answer is quite simple. Take a certain quantity and divide it into two parts, as you like. The quantity as such always remains the same, no matter how much of it is in one part or the other. Hence we must not consider only the one side, the earthly world; the other side too, the beyond, belongs to it. Of the total number of human spirits attaining to maturity on earth – which comprises those on this side and in the beyond – more and more are now being incarnated *here simultaneously*, because in view of the advanced state of the earth so many of them are still in need of this opportunity of late maturing.

To more than half of mankind on this globe of ours – to the whole of the Far East – reincarnation, even if to some extent in slightly distorted conceptions, is a foregone conclusion. Only we in the West think we must doubt it. But we do so against all reason. Do we not see the alternation in all the rhythms of Nature? There is summer and winter, day and night, ebb and flow, offshore and onshore winds, development and decay, blossom and fruit, fruit and seed. Always one thing stipulates the other. We too bear this Law within us: Breathing in compels us to breathe out, breathing out compels us to breathe in. Every beat of our heart pumps out blood and sucks it back; it circulates continuously from the systemic to the pulmonary side, back and forth, the sides constantly interchanging. And all these manifestations trace the form of a wave, mathematically they follow the sine curve, forming alternately an upward and a downward arc. But wherever this arc intersects the straight line of the zero-axis, the crossover point represents a change from one side to the other and vice versa.

Birth and death are nothing but such crossover points in the rhythm of human existence: Birth into earth-life is death in the beyond; earthly death, however, is birth on to the other side.

But if, in spite of what I have said to you earlier about the value of earthly proofs with regard to these matters, you should still ask for proofs, may I say to you: Direct this question to those who deny rebirth! On the side of those who are convinced about rebirth is the logic of the Laws of Life; let the others try to furnish proof that just here life acts *against* the universally valid Laws. But such a proof can never be given, because these Laws are adamantine and uniform.

Reincarnation has also been compatible with Christianity from the very beginning – which may surprise many. We read in the New Testament how at that time people variously assumed John the Baptist and Jesus to be the prophet Elijah reborn. But Elijah lived in the 9th century before Christ. The evangelists also report that there was talk among the people about a rebirth of the prophet Jeremiah. The latter, however, lived in the 7th century before Christ. Jesus certainly rejected these assumptions with regard to His person – but not by any means the idea of rebirth. On the contrary: the Evangelist Matthew even believes Jesus to have confirmed that John the Baptist was Elijah reborn (Matth. 11, 11-14 and 17, 10-13).

And please open your Bible at John 9, 1 - 3. There we read:

"And as Jesus passed by, he saw a man which was blind from his birth. And his disciples asked Him, saying, Master, who did sin, this man, or his parents, that he was born blind?"

But how can someone have sinned before his birth? The question asked by the disciples certainly points – not necessarily in doubt but as a possible cause – to guilt from a *former* life and therefore logically to that life itself. The question is based on the knowledge of reincarnation and the fateful connections ensuing from it. And how does Jesus react? Must He not reject this question because of its absurdity, must He not perhaps say: "How could you think such a thing?" But nothing of the kind happens. Jesus gives an objective reply, containing both alternatives. He says: "Neither hath this man sinned, nor his parents: but that the works of God should be made manifest in him" – thus referring to the healing of the blind man which took place afterwards.

As is well known, the Gospels were written only long after the death of Jesus. Yet it was not considered necessary to omit these clear references to rebirth, to express them differently or at least to explain them. This proves that the knowledge of rebirth still survived even after the time of Jesus.

In fact, in the theology of Origen, who – and I quote here from the encyclopaedia – "was the greatest scholar and by far the most prolific theological writer of his time, and moreover of the whole church before Augustine" – we find also the concept of the correlation of several lives and their interdependence.

This knowledge of reincarnation is essential if we are to be able to grasp our human existence as a *complete whole*. Without this knowledge we fare as one who would judge the action of a play, a film or a novel only on the basis of a single scene or chapter of it. He is bound to come to wrong conclusions, because he lacks the knowledge of the connections.

Hence we read in The Grail Message "In the Light of Truth":

"But one of the chief mistakes so many people make is that they judge only according to gross matter, regarding themselves as the centre in it, and taking into consideration **one** *earth-life, whereas in reality they already have several earth-lives behind them. These, as well as the intervening times in the Ethereal World, are equal to one* **uniform** *existence, through which the threads are tightly stretched without breaking, so that in the effects of a particular earthly existence only a small part of these threads therefore becomes visible.*

"Hence it is a great mistake to believe that at birth an absolutely new life begins, that a child is thus "innocent", and that all happenings can be accounted for in only the short life on earth. If this were true, then the existing Justice would naturally require the combined causes, effects and reactions to take place within the span of one earth-life.

"Turn away from this error. You will then soon discover in everything that happens the logic and justice which at present are so often missed!"

And from this we must now come to the conclusion that we have all lived repeatedly on earth before! For a long time now, because of the advanced ripeness of this celestial body, no one has been born here for the first time any more!

We must ask ourselves, then, how it could happen that the knowledge of reincarnation, which evidently existed in Christianity in the beginning, is no longer taught today. To that end let me recount some historical facts, which unfortunately are far too little known.

Long after the death of Origen, the Christian world was convulsed by severe conflicts. These concerned above all the question of whether Jesus had been God-man in *one* person or God *and* man, thus uniting *two* natures within Himself. Although it may seem incomprehensible to us today that people would arrogate the decision on such a question to themselves, yet at that time this conflict of opinion – in connection with the interpretation given by council resolutions which were later recorded in history as the so-called "Three Chapters Controversy" – shook the political unity of the Roman Empire. In his writings the long deceased Origen had supported the monophysitic doctrine, the concept of the one-fold nature of Jesus, which was fiercely opposed by the so-called Diophysites, the adherents of the twofold nature. As a result of these disturbances some provinces were finally even threatening to secede. For this reason the Emperor Justinian I convoked an Ecumenical Council, which finally met in Constantinople in 553. The Emperor sought to offer each of the opposing parties a favourable outcome by means of a twofold decision. Since the Monophysites cited Origen, he was to be anathematised as a heretic, and his teaching rejected, to satisfy the Diophysites. In return the Monophysites, through a decision agreeable to them in the "Three Chapters Controversy", were to emerge as victors.

To this end *the Emperor*, who at the same time regarded himself as the highest ecclesiastical authority – it was the age of the most pronounced imperial papalism, combining secular and ecclesiastical authority – the Emperor *himself* dictated those resolutions which the Ecumenical Council had to pass, including the one by which the entire works of Origen were to be anathematised. The Pope – it was Vigilius I – refused for more than six months to sign the resolutions of the Council and thereby make them binding on the whole church. As a result he was detained in Constantinople by the Emperor, and only allowed to leave the city after, in two letters addressed to the Emperor, he had taken a standpoint which at least came close to the Council's resolutions.

I have related this to you more fully because, in my opinion, what is in question here is one of the greatest tragedies in western spiritual history. For here a *decision on a matter of faith* of the greatest significance was *enforced* by *secular* authority solely out of political expediency. Through the condemning of Origen's works altogether – which was done without any relation to the question of reincarnation – reference to the succession of several lives, mutually conditioned by the basic Laws of Cause, Effect and Reaction, was also eliminated from the resources of Christian faith.

Thus we drag with us like a spiritual shackle the legacy of Justinian and his time. For the denial of reincarnation has cut man off from the knowledge of the great meshwork of his existence. It makes him question the continuance of his ego, the outliving of his physical existence; it conceals from us the purpose of life, and makes us doubt the Justice of God. For if we proceed from *this* birth as the origin of life, must it not seem unjust that the one is born rich, the other poor; the one healthy, the other sickly? And even the scientists stand perplexed before the question of how it is that human beings are so undeniably different. The assumption that environmental factors are decisive for this has proved to be right only in certain conditions. Above all twin research, especially in the case of identical twins who grew up apart in quite different circumstances, has all too clearly refuted such a view. The similar nature even of such people, extending to the last details in their behaviour, idiosyncracies and interests, has pointed to a similarity in natural inclinations even from birth. Should heredity therefore be decisive? In that case however our personality would then be all the more a product of chance, of arbitrariness. Hence this world, which is undeniably controlled by lawful principles – as for instance the Nobel prize-winner Manfred Eigen says: "The *oneness* of Nature manifests in its *Laws*" – hence this world, which is governed by Laws, would confront us from the very beginning with only a meaningless injustice, if we were to take as a basis this *one* earth-life alone!

With reincarnation, man held the key to all these questions in his hands long ago, but heedlessly threw it away. It is high time for us to rediscover it at last!

Of course some people simply shy away from concerning themselves with the idea of reincarnation, because they fear the responsibility connected with it. If everything ends with earthly death, many things must remain unatoned for. If however there is an after-life and rebirth, the circumstances of our next life will of course be shaped by the good qualities we bring with us, but also by our faults and weaknesses and all those ties clinging to us from former earth-lives, which are yet to be severed. That frightens many a person. But the Laws of Creation will not change, whether or not we wish to acknowledge them. Rather is it all the more necessary to face the facts and adjust our behaviour accordingly.

For it is just by the example of rebirth that we can see how much the human spirit urges to ever faster, ever richer development, inasmuch as it has already passed the primitive stage. How much the possibility of experiencing has grown by leaps and bounds from generation to generation, through the medium of communication. Yet what utter injustice there would be in the differing life-content of the former and present earth-dwellers if, yes if, we had not all lived through these earlier stages as well!

But this multiplicity of the things assailing us also demands an ever greater activity of the spirit. For it is not just a question of assimilating this wealth of experience intellectually, to say nothing of being crushed by it. What matters is to gain from it recognition of the working of the Eternal Laws which sustain this Creation, which permeate it, take effect in all happenings, and thereby become discernible to us. Unaffected by the changeable views of man, the *immovable Will of God* manifests in them. We must learn to understand It, to advance spiritually.

Much of what I have explained to you so far seemed to be not directly concerned with the *coming-into-being* of man, mentioned in the lecture title. But with good reason we are told in the Grail Message:

> "*You* ***must*** *lift your eyes far* ***beyond*** *this earth, and recognise where your path leads after this earthly life, so that at the same time you may become aware of why and for what purpose you are here on this earth.*"

Thus I hope you will understand that until we can recognise the full significance of our *being man,* a significance by no means limited to this one earth-life, we are unable to deal in the right sense with the *coming-into-being* of man. Only now are we in a position to fit it into the wider context, where it belongs.

And now we stand before the fact that really there is no "human being" at all; there are only men and women. This plays an important part in the very coming-into-being of man. Here the different tasks cannot be overlooked. But over and above that, people today think that the sexes can be standardised. One hears ever more frequently that the different spheres of interest are merely an "inculcated behaviour in a particular role". Give the train-set to the girl, the doll's kitchen to the boy to play with, and the specifically sex-linked inclinations would be lost. This alarmingly expresses the human arrogance which, ignorant of the ordained purpose, presumptuously attempts to change the realities of Creation.

For not only has the difference between the sexes to do with their role in the reproductive process, it is rooted in the spirit. Within it lies an order of gradation, testifying to the Wisdom and Love of the Creator, a kind of "development-aid" for the human spirit.

Man's field of activity is coarser, more down-to-earth; in short, he is more closely bound up with the earth than woman. He also has the appropriate equipment for this, in the greater robustness of his body. The working of the woman, on the other hand, lies in caring, tending, in activities related to the natural. It is determined by finer stirrings, which also manifests in her physical structure. Concepts such as grace and charm are really vested in the womanly. Thus woman, through the nature of her being which is rooted in the spirit, forms the bridge to a finer world; she stands a little nearer to that more permeable world than man. Through this alone it is her task – quite unconsciously – to keep awake also in him, the one nearer to the earth, the longing for higher things.

Through her nature, woman becomes an incentive for man to refine and ennoble himself. The very presence of a true woman is often able to bring this about. It is with good reason that Goethe says in "Tasso":

"And if you would know what is seemly, ask of noble women!"

Man quite rightly senses that it is his allotted task – a task that moves him joyfully to unfold his highest virtues, thus consideration, chivalry and manly courage – to protect the noble, that is the true woman, who has preserved her womanly nature, from the hardships of this coarse world. Upon this is based the concept of woman as the "weaker sex", a concept which has been devalued and misunderstood. Yet seen from the spiritual it is just in this somewhat looser connection with coarsest matter that the furthering power, the strength of woman, lies. Naturally it is strength of a different kind from that of man.

For this reason it is utterly wrong when the endeavour to obtain equal rights for woman, which unfortunately has become necessary in our modern world, is directed towards increasingly opening up masculine fields of activity for her. Undoubtedly she is able to fill also these positions, but in many cases only by repressing her womanly personality, and above all at the cost of over-straining herself, since generally she is still not spared the womanly tasks of caring for her own. Therefore we are going in exactly the wrong direction when here too the masculine activity is again made the measure for the supposed "raising" of woman's status, instead of the same respect at last being offered to her work which is different in nature.

In reflecting on how this should come about, you must not use today's economic and social order as a basis. This order is the result of human misconduct. From the spiritual things can only be described as they *should* be, according to the Will of the *Creator.*

Therefore I have had to bring again to your awareness the lofty task which, in accordance with the Creation-plan, falls to the share of woman for the spiritual upliftment of mankind. For in misunderstanding, denying, indeed withdrawing from this task, which can now be frequently observed, lies the real cause of the numerous complications with regard to the relationship between partners, and also the coming-into-being of man. This bridge upwards into the finer, the less material, which is given to humanity in the form of woman, serves not only the ennoblement of man, but also the entry of new human life. I would remind you, as I have already said earlier, that everything in Creation is based on radiation.

"*For there is life only in radiation, and only in* and through radiation *is movement generated*".

So we read in the Grail Message, and I ask you to consider in its effects just this one sentence, which is not refuted by any scientific recognition. Hence follows something that is also of quite decisive importance for the coming-into-being of man: For only across the refined *radiation-bridge* formed by the nature of the female spirit can a human spirit that is meant for embodiment reach this earthly world; coming from the world beyond, thus from the less dense world, the spirit needs this radiation-like transition. Do not forget that in fact everything forms as it becomes denser, coming from above from the lighter and finer.

Therefore looking at things differently for once, that is from the spiritual, the fact that only woman possesses the organs that serve the development of a human body is only the material manifestation, the effect of her mediator-role, which is based on the feminine spiritual nature. But of no less importance is the radiation-bridge formed through this. If it is decayed or even destroyed through the woman becoming masculine, through an incisive change in her nature, then difficult pregnancies, premature births, indeed even infertility may be the outcome. Hence the cause of such complaints can certainly lie even in the spiritual. For man will not alter without ill-effect what has been ordained by the Wisdom of God. Therefore it will never be possible to produce human life in the test-tube. The radiation of the feminine is needed. Even the so-called "test-tube babies" had to be carried to full time by a woman after fertilisation in the test-tube.

Only when man has become clear that the sexual is rooted in the spiritual will he also draw nearer to the significance of the generative power. The idea that it is meant, indeed allowed, to serve only the purpose of procreation belittles it to something gross-material, functional. Of much greater importance is this ability to the spirit.

During the years of childhood, while the physical body is maturing, this spirit lives sheltered as though behind a rampart. The instrument which it may use in this life is still incomplete. That means (remember the sentence about radiations which was quoted earlier): The radiation of the spirit does not yet encompass the complete radiation-spectrum of this earthly world, it is not yet fully open to it, and therefore cannot yet completely link with it. The child is predominantly inclined to the natural, he lives through the early development stages of mankind. He bears no responsibility yet for earthly events. Our legal system expresses this quite rightly: To begin with the child is under age, afterwards a minor. Others have to act on his behalf. His own ability to act, and also his full responsibility, set in only when he has come of age. What has taken place? Sexual maturity has set in, and as can be seen, it has a very practical meaning. It is as though a drawbridge had been lowered, over which the spirit only now attains to the complete connection with the outside world. Now acting responsibly, it steps out into the world, but is also exposed to its influences. The actual significance of the generative power lies in providing the spirit with this full reciprocal binding into the earthly world. It is the most mature expression of which the material body is capable. It is the vital energy of the adult earth-man. We make use of it in all our doings, not only in sexual activity.

If now the two parts of the creature "man", hence man and woman – which though different are called to complementary activity – strive towards one another, are attracted to each other like opposite poles in physics, the spiritual bond of love should establish the connection between them. One is almost ashamed of still having to emphasise something so self-evident. But our modern age has transposed the signs, and placed the material-instinctive, coveting "sex" in the forefront. It is the very opposite of love, which comes from the spirit. Love's significance reaches far beyond liking and harmony, it lies in the spiritual advancement of the partners. Only through this can the relationship between the partners fulfil its true, higher purpose. For love indeed offers the strongest aid to spiritual ascent. Without compulsion it makes us exercise consideration and selflessness, disregarding our own ego in favour of the other. For through love a voluntary, joyful volition to serve comes to life. With that man grows into his task in Creation, he learns to adapt himself in the fullest sense, and recognises that only in giving can there also be receiving.

Only then does this love, which is meant for the spirit of the other, for his whole being, seek to find its release through the body, because this body-covering is simply the outer shell, the vessel of the beloved spirit. Then nothing unclean, nothing immoral attaches to all this. For it can never be wrong to use the gift bestowed by the Creator in a natural way, since it makes possible something which serves the gladdening complement of the partners: the exchange of ethereal fluid forces. Therefore we find in the Grail Message this sentence, which is so immensely important for the understanding of the generative power:

"The purpose of procreation comes only in the **second** *place."*

Now it may be that two partners who are so united with one another "wish for a child", that they "want to have a child". But do you notice how much these common expressions refer to the parents? This reflects our radically wrong attitude to the question of descendants. And if a child gets lost somewhere in a crowd, the question "To whom does the child belong?" will most certainly be asked. But the child does not "belong" to anyone – only to himself. He is not acquired like a piece of property. He is no toy. He is an independent human spirit who, just like his parents, has already journeyed through many lives. What distinguishes him from his parents is simply the fact that his physical body must first be trained, and – as explained before – only out of a certain maturity of this body can his spirit work fully in an outward direction.

Anyone who sees in the child an employee, a provider, and already has designs on him from an early age, will and must be disappointed. For the child has to tread his *own* path of spiritual development. He must experience what is of benefit to *himself* – not to his parents. Every disregard of this principle would be a transgression of the Fifth Commandment. Let us not blinker ourselves by imagining that "killing" relates only to the physical. It does not say so anywhere. From the spiritual standpoint – and it is from this that our existence is to be examined here – every obstacle with which we hinder the spiritual development of another, every suppression of his just possibilities of unfolding, is a "killing" that certainly also includes a deadening.

We are told in the Grail Message what should actually be the basis of the wish for a child. And I ask you here to pay strict attention to every word! For tremendously important things are contained in these few sentences. It says there:

> *"For spiritually free human beings procreation should be nothing but the proof of their willingness to take a strange human spirit into the family as a permanent guest, offering it the opportunity to atone and to mature on earth. Only when both sides have the fervent wish* **to achieve this purpose** *should the opportunity for procreation be sought."*

Does not this happening thereby take on a completely different, much greater dimension? Do we not first learn through this to understand the meaning of the procreative ability given to us? These words make clear what the coming-into-being of man really means spiritually. There is no more room for the selfish wishes of parents who "want to have a child". Here this wonderful power of helpful love is of *service* to another spirit-creature. An all-embracing Commandment of Creation can be realised here, namely to love one's neighbour as oneself, that is to say, to make possible for him what each one should himself strive for as the highest: to advance on the road to spiritual maturity!

Reciprocally this striving will then bring spiritual gain to the parents too. Indeed the trouble, the care which they take over the child, the joy it gives them, also mean intense experiencing, and make it possible for them to sever many a – perhaps very old – entanglement. For the "strange" guest spoken of earlier is in most cases by no means so strange. Its coming to just these or those parents does not take place arbitrarily, but – as is yet to be discussed – on the basis of wise Laws.

To become aware of this spiritual significance to parents and child of man's coming-into-being is fundamentally necessary in order to be able to solve all further questions associated with it in accordance with the Laws of Creation. –

While one woman regards a child as unwanted and does everything to prevent a pregnancy, another falls into the opposite extreme. Her whole life, as we say, "is entirely devoted to motherhood"; in it she sees her highest goal, her fulfilment. This is also wrong, for it is too little. Motherhood is the noblest flower of the natural, I should like to say "animistic" qualities of woman. But the maternal in itself is also characteristic of the female animal. It is not something that would be reserved for the human woman if this motherhood did not also embrace the spiritual significance of the coming-into-being of man, thus becoming a spiritual help also for the mother. Indeed there is a gradation-order in all this. The generative power was the most mature outworking of the physical *body,* motherhood is the noblest form of activity of the *female-natural;* the two, building up on each other, prepare the earthly foundation for the entry of the *spirit*, which stands above them. And now you can see that because the spirit stands above these, the mother too has to tread *her* spiritual path. For that is why she is on earth. She may see in motherhood only a high possibility that helps her to achieve her goal, but not the goal itself, nor the purpose of her life.

In the words of the Grail Message quoted earlier, it was said that procreation should take place only where the spiritual wish exists on *both* sides. Hence this means that on this point man not only may, but even *should* make a decision; indeed a harmonious decision of will made by both parents is demanded. For the coming-into-being of man is much too important an event to make it independent of the volition of man as a spirit-creature. It is a matter of *knowingly* assuming responsibility for the benefit of another as yet unknown. But how much harm, what mental anguish has been brought about by the denial of this freedom of decision, which after all is really self-evident by virtue of human dignity alone!

Of course at the same time it must be noted that our will is not always done, that out of higher necessity it may not always be done. For the words of the Grail Message quoted earlier referred to the "spiritually free" human being. That is only he whose will is not already bound in this respect through still outstanding reactions from former decisions of will. Therefore only that man who lives in accordance with the Laws of God is truly free. Wherever he does something which transgresses the Laws of Nature, in short which is unnatural, he will incur consequences, and with them ties. Today this principle of reaction, of reciprocal action, which holds good in everything, has even been recognised by scientists as a Law of Nature. On account of his previous life-journeys, his former earth-lives, every human being is exposed to such reactions from erstwhile wrong decisions. As a result of this, because of these already existing ties, something which he does not like, which he seeks to avoid, has to take place now and then. But this never happens to our detriment. What takes place in this connection is always only that which benefits us *spiritually*, which helps us to sever still existing entanglements and thereby to mature. But at present, owing to our limited vision, we are frequently unable as yet to perceive it.

Hence even if we are allowed to make decisions with regard to birth-control, indeed are meant to do so – for every decision is a process of maturing on a small scale – their realisation must remain within the Laws of God. Therefore many a possibility open to man today, through which he believes he can be absolved of obligations, efforts and cares, implies a fateful tie for the future. This will always be the case when he acts against Nature.

In order to understand this concept aright, take as a guiding principle this sentence from the Grail Message:

> *"To be natural means to listen attentively to one's intuitive perceptions and not forcibly to disregard their warnings."*

So much for this vast subject. It is not possible, for the purpose of this lecture, to go into details. I would like only to single out something particularly incisive, namely that in several countries today legislation allows the termination of pregnancy during the first three months after conception. Even though this is not punishable under human law, it does not mean that it would also be without consequences under the Laws of Creation.

Just in connection with attempts to determine the time-limit, the liveliest debates on when human life actually begins have taken place. Some say, already at procreation; and others, only at birth. And finally, without any compelling reasons for it, a time-limit of three months after conception was agreed on.

Yet there is very definitely an exact time in the course of this coming-into-being of man when a fundamental change manifests quite clearly. It is that moment when for the first time the expectant mother distinctly feels the child's movements in her body. This point is about half way through pregnancy. Now the incarnation has taken place. That is to say, a human spirit has taken possession of the developing body.

Do you still remember the description I gave you of the first coming-into-being of man on earth? Of the most highly evolved animal body, which only through the entry of the spirit was able to continue its development into the human body?

With the coming-into-being of every single man, the reflection of that happening which once allowed mankind to arise here on earth is repeated. Here at the apex, at the mid-point of pregnancy, the development process hitherto cared for only from the Material World has reached its peak. The addition of the spirit is needed to continue the development into man.

But how does the entry of the spirit come about? Please recall what I said in the beginning about the radiation-connection of spirit, soul and body. Not until the middle of pregnancy has the radiation of the developing body-covering attained to that strength which enables it to hold fast the spirit with its finer coverings, in short the soul. It is drawn into the body by this radiation. Only through this is the spirit now able to take possession of the developing body, to make use of it, to move it. If by the concept "man" we understand this connection of spirit and body into one unit, we could then assume that the creature "earth-man" begins to exist only at the moment of incarnation, hence in the middle of pregnancy.

But this does not mean that until then the developing child's body may be treated arbitrarily, or as an object. Although the spirit is not yet within the body, connections between the two already exist.

For the incarnating spirit does not just suddenly drop into the prepared body. It is a smooth, slowly intensifying process – and that is why science can hardly find a discernible boundary here.

The incarnation of the spirit also refutes the widespread opinion that parents could "give life" to their child. The spirit attaining to embodiment had life long before that – it received it from its Creator. But the parents can "call" it into earthly existence – if it is still in need of such an earth-life.

This call begins already with procreation. Through the union of egg and sperm-cell a new radiation-combination arises, which goes out like the call of a transmitter frequency and is received by one who is tuned in to the same frequency. It is the same principle which we find again in coarser form in technology involving transmitter and receiver. Today we are no longer surprised that it is possible to send signals to the Moon, Mars and Venus using quite weak impulses, and to transmit commands to space probes. Now the call that goes forth from the radiation-connection during procreation attracts the corresponding spirit, which by virtue of an inner relationship responds to the nature of this vibration, like the effect that the call-note of animals brings about on a much coarser plane in Nature.

This process is described to us very impressively in the Grail Message:

"Just realise that in the immediate beyond a great number of souls are standing ready and awaiting the opportunity to reincarnate on earth. They are mostly such human souls, held fast by threads of karma, as are seeking some atonement in a new earth-life.

"As soon as an opportunity is presented, they attach themselves to where an act of procreation has taken place, in order to await and follow up the growth of the new human body as a dwelling. During this waiting period ethereal threads are then spun from the young body to the soul – which stays persistently quite close to the prospective mother – and from the soul to the young body; and at a definite stage of maturity these threads then serve as the bridge to admit the alien soul from the beyond to the young body, which it immediately claims for itself."

Perhaps you can now more readily imagine how important an intervention in this happening is. Consider that everything which begins to form in the body, hence physically, must first have a finer prototype, the astral model. Therefore any interference produces effects above and beyond the body of the woman. Through this the astral model for its body is destroyed even before the entry of the spirit; radiation-threads that have formed between the waiting spirit and the developing body are torn.

Surely in our earthly business life it would hardly occur to the owner of a factory to destroy an article which is being manufactured there, and has already been promised to a customer, on the authority of his proprietary right to this factory. At any rate he would realise that by such conduct he would be damaging the other person's interests, and become liable for damages.

How then can we imagine that a termination of pregnancy would not entail any responsibility? As I have said already, the Fifth Commandment must not only be interpreted materially. It embraces any kind of deadening, even that of hopes, talents, possibilities of development. In the case of abortion, the hope of a human spirit for an earth-life that was to offer him redemption and spiritual advancement is destroyed, killed. Moreover, even the parents thereby rob themselves of the possibility of karmaic redemption, which however they cannot be spared. It is merely postponed, and only made still more difficult through the fresh new entanglement.

It is never just by chance that a spirit is incarnated with certain parents; there is a purpose behind it. Either a fateful entanglement, that is to say one from previous lives, still awaiting redemption, brings about such a connection; or else one of the fundamental Laws of Creation is decisive for the incarnation, namely the Law of *Attraction of Homogeneous Species*, which likewise offers the parties concerned the opportunity to mature through one another.

And a few things must again be said about this, because here also the lack of knowledge of the spiritual has led to erroneous views. If a child has interests, talents, abilities that were already present in a parent he is often said to have inherited these from his father or his mother. And that is wrong. For there is no heredity in the spiritual, because each spirit is independent in itself, and has travelled its own particular path of development. *Its* experiences, *its* decisions and their reactions have formed it, and brought it to that position which it now occupies at the beginning of its new life.

When we say "birds of a feather flock together", we mean by it this very Law of the Attraction of Homogeneous Species, which brings together those who, as people say, "get on well" because they have similar dispositions. But this "getting on well" is something non-physical. Hence it concerns a spiritual homogeneity, which makes them "vibrate on the same wavelength". The social circle a man belongs to, the many associations, are all based on this fact. "A man is known by the company he keeps" means that from this homogeneity we can even draw a conclusion about a man's personality. But the people with whom he associates, with whom he meets in a club, are not related to him. Why then should we think that it would be a question of heredity when just such a spiritual homogeneity occurs between parents and children? The proverb "like father, like son", frequently used in this connection, refers in fact to nothing other than simply this Law of the Attraction of Spiritually Homogeneous Species.

Therefore please note that here there is a decisive line of demarcation. Heredity exists only in the physical; in the spiritual operates the much more far-reaching Law of the Attraction of Homogeneous Species, which we wrongly regard as heredity simply because we know hardly anything of the spirit. Man can inherit blond hair, blue eyes, a birth-mark, or protruding ears – this remains in the material, where the Mendelian Laws apply; but never anything that is rooted in the condition of the spirit.

Certainly the spirit in the main forms the body. From this arise also physical similarities between parents and children – but often with total strangers too. You will be able to observe that this quality of a "double" is not restricted to the external appearance only, but embraces the whole being: the manner of conduct, of speaking, as well as the interests. Here too there is no heredity, but a homogeneity of spirit, which fashions similar body-forms.

And through this the incarnating spirit also finds exactly those conditions that correspond to it, which on account of its nature it requires for its further spiritual development.

So for instance, through the attraction of homogeneous species, a selfish, greedy man will be born where greed and selfishness likewise hold sway. Hence he will have to suffer under these characteristics. In this lies not only justice, which now allows him to experience what he formerly inflicted on others, but at the same time also helping love, which seeks to help him to change and become discerning through suffering from his own faults. In the same way, the spirit that has already developed good qualities in previous lives also finds an opportunity to advance and develop them further through this attraction of homogeneous species.

In The Grail Message "In the Light of Truth" we read:

"This attraction power of all that is of the same nature, which is so important in the birth of a child, can proceed from the father, from the mother, or from anyone in the vicinity of the expectant mother. **Therefore an expectant mother ought to be very careful whom she allows around her.** *Consideration must be given to the fact that it is not in the outward character, but primarily in one's* **weaknesses** *that inner strength lies. Weaknesses bring important periods of inner experiencing which produce a strong power of attraction."*

With this we are again told something that is of enormous importance in two ways. The very aspects of our personality that still need improvement because they are not in accord with the Laws of God, hence those which in loving extenuation we call "weaknesses", because here we have not yet gained the strength to confront our wrong desiring victoriously, are just those aspects that can manifest decisively in the attraction of homogeneous species. For the yielding in the face of these weaknesses, and the ensuing struggle with oneself, leads to particularly strong experiencing.

But you have also heard that the *surroundings* of the mother can play an important part in the process. If through the parents' lack of care this alien radiation prevails, it can bring a disturbance into the lawful course of the happening. It is then as though a jamming station were being imposed on the parents' own frequency. This explains why now and then a so-called "black sheep" can come into an otherwise good family.

All this makes clear the high responsibility that devolves on the parents in the spiritual sense with the coming-into-being of man. For inasmuch as fateful entanglements are not bound to take effect, parents can make a kind of choice from among the human spirits possible for an incarnation, through their spiritual attitude and through paying attention to their surroundings, and in this way protect themselves from a guest who is perhaps not very pleasant.

You have of course heard of this Law of Attraction of Homogeneous Species. But when you think about it a little you will probably come up against a so-called contradiction. For do we not also say: "Opposites attract one another"? And do we not find this also confirmed in the manifestations of this world? Which, then, holds good? Therefore let me enter into this as well, because either is right. For this too the Grail Message offers us the explanation: Wherever there is a splitting-up into polarities, such as plus / minus – active / passive – male / female – these opposites attract one another because characteristic of such *split* species is the desire to join together in a complementary way. But to the species *complete* in themselves applies the Law of Attraction of Homogeneous Species. Hence mankind, for example, is split into men and women. Between them comes into effect the desire for union of the split species. The qualities of a human being, on the other hand, such as self-seeking, avarice, the love of Nature, musicality and countless others besides, in short his inclinations, interests and abilities, are all species complete in themselves which have an attracting effect on their homogeneous species.

To what abnormalities the lack of knowledge of these hidden connections gives rise has been clearly demonstrated quite recently in the form of "surrogate mothers". I refer particularly to this instance: A couple who are denied offspring in the natural way allow the egg to be fertilised in the test-tube, implanted in and carried for the full time by another woman. In such a way the coming-into-being of man is debased to a functional, matter-of-course production-process, in the legal sense to a kind of work-contract. They have a child "manufactured" from donated material. Those who imagine that they can acquire a child "of their own" by this roundabout method – and this is the endeavour behind it – labour under a delusion. The child may outwardly exhibit some similarity or other to them. But the spirit within – and after all, it is the essence of man – will bring with it those qualities, weaknesses and tendencies which could similarly be found in the "surrogate mother" or those around her.

But in all this lies also the explanation of the ever-spreading decline of our world, of the increase in crime and violence. Indifference towards the so important event of the coming-into-being of man; ignorance of the spiritual responsibility involved; carelessness about the company man keeps; thoughts which move in the world of crime and immorality just for the pleasure of sensation (we need only think of cinema, television and press), and finally the life-style, with its emphasis on materialistic interests – all these can only lead to ever more spirits reaching the earth, who bring with them even from previous lives a lack of moral responsibility, and greed for material things.

Without the knowledge of these actual causes, which lie in the spiritual, men are readily inclined to assume that the Creator is responsible for the deplorable state of this modern world of ours. They feel that there is no justice, and think there is a blind senselessness in the distribution of births, whose inequality must be levelled as far as possible by a "socially" regarded legislation. But one sentence of the Grail Message – connected with the knowledge of rebirth – can solve all these problems:

> *"The inequality among men is only the inevitable consequence of their own free will",*

of their decisions of will from former lives!

In the working of the immutable Laws of God there is no injustice. Just as a key proves useful only for the lock that fits it, because only there can it work in its own way, so also in each case the conditions into which an incarnating spirit is placed offer the appropriate development-possibilities for this particular spirit. But even in this graphic example – and in it you can see how it corresponds to the responsibility of the parents just mentioned – it is the lock that determines which key will fit.

Hence the environment into which a man is born is, so to speak, the launching pad which he has prepared for himself from the sum total of his previous lives for this continuing life-journey. Whither this journey is to lead then rests with himself. For all fateful entanglements can again be redeemed through the firm volition for the good, for the rightly-understood spiritual ascent. That indeed is the wonderful comfort contained in these Laws. Alas, for the purpose of this lecture it is not possible to enter into this more fully. But helps upon helps are at our disposal if only, through understanding these Laws, we learn at last to make use of their furthering effect. After all, any of the inventions of which we are so proud are only based on the utilisation of these Laws. Why then do we hesitate to do the same also in the spiritual?

For we can certainly obtain answers to these questions before which we stand rather helpless, and really uneasy, when we have to make decisions in the consciousness that we do not have at all the right criterion of right or wrong. For as I have cited at the beginning, even the experts concede "but of man we know nothing". Therefore we cannot expect any clarification from them. Do not the words of the Grail Message then sound more than justified:

"But how foolish you are, you men, how narrowly you have constricted your outlook on everything, particularly on that which concerns **you** *and your wanderings through the Creations."*

Therefore let us at last burst the narrow limitations of our field of vision! Let us follow the instruction of the Grail Message:

"Become **spiritual** *at last, you men, for you are of the spirit!"*

You will, I hope, have observed that in the course of this contemplation I have not in the least altered the well-known phenomena, the findings, established by science. I have only included the spiritual which hitherto has remained unheeded. And all at once those facts that stood alone, leaving numerous unsolved questions, appear in a meaningful context.

Yet it was only a small facet that I could offer you; but it covered a range of topics which certainly concerns us all as human beings, and which has especially filled our minds in recent years. Much more could be said about it, for I have only been able to show the hidden connections in broad outline. And even with these many a thing may have sounded new, unfamiliar, perhaps even strange to you. But free yourselves from rigid, encrusted thought-patterns! Just in our time we are faced again and again with the necessity to re-think. Fresh insights are blazing a trail.

"The new world-vision calls upon us to abandon many of our deep-rooted world-views, our firmly held ideas."

So says for instance, like many others, the American atomic physicist Gary Zukav – and this refers not only to natural science. The call rings out from all sides. We must increasingly learn to fit our splintered, fragmented recognitions into a great, comprehensive order. We are being forced into holistic thinking. It is a thinking that is no longer satisfied with outward appearances, but includes the interweaving at work behind them. This applies all the more to our humanity and purpose of existence, from which just the decisive factor – the spirit and its development – can no longer be excluded.

In this connection nothing more is demanded of you than finally to step across that wretched, obstructive threshold erected by scepticism, which prevents so many people from recognising themselves as spiritual creatures, and our existence as a vast, purposeful whole.

If you are ready for such a comprehensive expansion of your world-view, if you are a human being who honestly seeks the Truth, then I may refer you to the Book I have repeatedly mentioned before, *"In the Light of Truth" The Grail Message by Abd-ru-shin.* For it is not I who have presumed to be able to give you enlightenment about humanity's problems. Only the way in which I have tried to convey them to you, only the bridges that I have built for you stem from me. If perhaps you should think that I have sometimes over-simplified things by giving you examples from everyday events in our lives, you are quite right! For all that is great and true is simple, and this simplicity entails discovering this truth again everywhere. First however, our eyes must be opened for it. And this is the invaluable merit of him who has written this Work and explained to us in it the Laws of Creation, Creation itself and our path therein. The obvious question of where he obtained this knowledge is answered of itself through the Book.

But I have no illusions that my recommendation could be decisive for you – nor is it by any means intended to be. For the Author of the Grail Message does not wish you simply to adopt the opinions and assertions of others. He wants the conviction of its rightness to grow out of yourselves. Therefore even in the Foreword to his Work he writes:

"Conviction comes solely through an inflexible weighing and examining!"

Therefore make a start with it! Investigate whether what you have heard today does not seem to you at least worth pondering over.

In conclusion, one more word of clarification is called for, so that you do not misunderstand me; for in our modern age, so contaminated with commercialism, a certain scepticism unfortunately is often not out of place. You can of course obtain the Book I have mentioned if you so wish – but no one is interested in "selling it", as is already evident from the disproportionately low price alone, considering its size and quality. It is solely a matter of offering you this help. A help in solving your life's problems, in the search for GOD, which is often beset with so many doubts, with the answer to the question which after all is ultimately decisive, whether or no HE really exists.

If you should have perceived a little *of that* from my words, but above all from the words of the Grail Message, I shall be happy. The Author of the Grail Message has couched this aim in the words with which I should like to close my explanations, because in my opinion there is nothing more to add to them:

"In order to convey to mankind such knowledge, which gives them a clear and intelligible conviction of the working of God in His Justice and Love, I have written the Work 'In the Light of Truth', which leaves no gap, contains the answer to **every** *question, and clearly shows mankind how wonderful are the ways in Creation that are upheld by many servants of His Will."*

"Not a single question remains unsolved for you; a great understanding arises within you of the mysterious working of the adamantine Laws in Creation, which guide you with the outworkings of your volition; and as a crowning for your trouble comes the wonderful divining of a Wisdom, of an Omnipotence, of a Love and of a Justice that can only issue from **God***, Whose Being you therewith discover!"*

“In the Light of Truth”

The Grail Message by Abd-ru-shin

Among all books of spiritual content this Work occupies a unique place. It brings the recognition of the all-embracing Laws of Creation, and guides the reader to a profound knowledge of the meaning of existence.

The Author writes:
“... I wish to fill the gaps which have so far always remained unanswered in the souls of men, and which never leave any serious thinker in peace, if he honestly seeks the Truth.”

Edition in three Volumes:

Linen	
Volume I	208 pages
Volume II	412 pages
Volume III	456 pages

Edition in one Volume:

Skivertex	1062 pages

Original edition: German
Translations available:
English, French,
Italian, Dutch,
Portuguese, Spanish,
Czech

In preparation: Russian

The Grail Message "In the Light of Truth" contains the following lectures:

VOLUME I
For your guidance!
What seek ye?
The call for the helper
The Antichrist
Morality
Awake!
Silence
Ascent
Cult
Rigidity
Childlikeness
Chastity
The first step
The World
The Star of Bethlehem
The conflict
Modern psychic science
Wrong courses
What separates so many from the Light today?
Once upon a time...!
Errors
The human word
The woman of Subsequent Creation
Submission
Indolence of the spirit
Earthman before his God
All that is dead in Creation shall be awakened, so that it may pass judgment upon itself!
The Book of Life
The Millennium
A necessary word
The great Comet
The World Teacher
The Stranger
Salvation! Redemption!
The Language of the Lord

VOLUME II
Responsibility
Fate
The creation of man
Man in Creation
Hereditary sin
God
The inner voice
The religion of love
The Redeemer
The mystery of birth
Is occult training advisable?
Spiritism
Earthbound
Does sexual continence further spiritual development?
Thought-forms
Watch and pray!
Marriage
The claim of children on their parents
Prayer
The Lord's Prayer
The worship of God
Man and his free will
Ideal human beings
Cast all your guilt upon Him!
The crime of hypnotism
Astrology
Symbolism in the fate of man
Faith
Earthly possessions
Death
Departed this life!
Miracles
Baptism
The Holy Grail
The mystery of Lucifer
The regions of Darkness and Damnation
The regions of Light and Paradise
World events
The difference in origin of man and animal
The separation between mankind and science
Spirit
The development of Creation
I am the Lord thy God!
The immaculate conception and the birth of the Son of God
The crucifixion of the Son of God and the Lord's Supper
Come down from the Cross!
This is My body; this is My blood!
The resurrection of Christ's physical body
Human opinions and God's Will in the Law of Reciprocal Action
The Son of Man
The significance of man's generative power for his spiritual ascent
I am the Resurrection and the Life, no man cometh to the Father but by me!
Gross matter, ethereal matter, radiations, space and time
The error about clairvoyance
Various aspects of clairvoyance
In the realm of demons and phantoms
Occult training, meat diet or vegetable diet
Healing by magnetism
Live in the present!

The following are available to give information in their respective countries:

Australia:
The Grail Movement of Australia
Kalorama Chalet
Falls Road
Kalorama, Vic. 3766

Canada:
Grail Movement of Canada
C.P. 277
Shawinigan, (Québec)
G9N 6T9

Great Britain:
The Grail Message Foundation
PO Box 5181, Milton Keynes MK2 3ZG
Tel.: (0)1908 274256

New Zealand:
The Grail Movement in
New Zealand
P.O. Box 60042
Titirangi / Auckland

Nigeria:
Grail Movement – Nigeria
Grailland, Iju Hill
P.O. Box 4157
Lagos

USA:
Grail Foundation of America
2081 Partridge Lane
Binghamton
N.Y. 13903

Richard Steinpach, "Hidden Connections Determine our Earth-life". Second edition 1989.
Title of the original German edition: "Verborgene Zusammenhänge bestimmen unser Erdenleben". Owner of the copyrights Richard Steinpach, Vienna. Published under licence by the Stiftung Gralsbotschaft, Stuttgart, Federal Republic of Germany, and its Publishing Company.
Printed in Germany.